To Bettie
I am !
& am so happy
a part of our family !
Love you
tons!

To Thine Ownself

Be True:

Happy #1 !

A More-Than-*Just*-
Survival
Guide

Sandy

By Sandy Jolley

DEDICATION

I dedicate this book to my mom, Lou Jolley. I wish she had lived long enough to find resolution for her past. I love you, Mom, and miss you every day. Thanks for being my Mom. I am glad you became one of my best friends. You taught me so much more than I can ever say.

Table of Contents

Acknowledgements

Without recovery, I wouldn't be alive today. I am sure of that. I had so few coping skills when I started my journey and, long before I drank alcoholically, I just wanted to die. The pain caused by so many of my life experiences was my constant companion: past traumas, peer pressure, loss (with no way to grieve), internalized self-phobia, self-hatred, suicidal ideation, inability to cope with *any* feelings, and so many other things I just couldn't resolve on my own, were keeping me hostage in my own life.

I couldn't have gotten to where I am today without legions of people on my side. "We" is the first word of the first step of traditional 12 step programs, and there are so many people I owe my very life to in that "we". I can't possibly name them all, but there are some that must be named. To Ben Branch, my soul-mate, my bestest forever friend, the love of my life, and my companion in recovery; Suzanne Cepello, my sister, and one of my best friends forever, who I love dearly, and am so grateful to have in my life; Doris B, you will always be my mentor and role model; Jeanne Shilstone, one of my oldest and dearest friends, we have walked this journey for a long time together and apart (I am so glad we reconnected); Maggi O'C; Kitty M; Patricia M; Ellen McC; Kim M; Nanci Dotson; Tempy Albright; Mary Clark-Jackson, (my twin sister!); Tammy Dosier; Debbie Spencer; Preston Group, Dallas, TX; Lambda Group, Dallas, TX; Serenity Group Women's Meeting, Kernersville, NC; and all my friends in secular recovery online meetings. To all my therapists and the professionals who have directed me on my path and helped me to become my best me yet: Rachel Whelan; Charles Herndon; Peg Carter; Jan Pearce; Liz Moulin; Arlene Gold; Dr. Daniel Myers; and so many others over the years, I am very grateful.

To the most awesome, fantastic proof-reader ever, as well as a great sister-friend: Ruth Owens. You will never know how much you and thank you for understanding my intention; however, I am a little concerned that you felt so comfortable getting in my brain! LOL!!

To those who have encouraged me by their writing and their own recovery, I owe you a debt of gratitude: Earnie Larsen, Pia Mellody, Melody Beattie, John Bradshaw, Ellen Bass and Laura Davis, and too many more to list.

And ZOOM: In this time of COVID, ZOOM has become a way to stay connected, and continue growing and processing. I doubt the creators of Zoom know how important their communication tool has become or how many thousands of lives they have saved and enriched, just by being available any time day or night.

And, last, but certainly not least, to Bill W. and Dr. Bob S. Along with all the millions of others who have come before me, I thank you with all my heart. I hope that by sharing what I have learned, I may be able to help others on their paths of recovery.

Introduction and About the Author

What do you "need" to know about me? I don't know! What I can tell you about me, though, is that, as I write this, I am a recovering alcoholic, with over 36 years of sobriety. I stopped drinking in 1984, but that was just the beginning; my journey since getting sober has included many avenues. I have had ups and downs, and even a few all-arounds! I have discovered things I blocked from childhood, learned to make sense of things that made no sense, and chosen to face truths so painful I thought I would die. But, I haven't; at least not yet.

I use the words "choose" and "chose" frequently, as you will see. This is because, when I first got sober, I didn't know I had a choice. I only had reactions. I had very few ways to cope with things I couldn't process, other than denial, avoidance, and dismissal. I thought if I didn't look at it, the problem couldn't get me. But it always did; whatever the "it" was at the time. I have had lots of "it's". I think we all do. The "it" might be finances, body distortion, feelings we don't know how to manage or express, fear of the loss of possessions, fear of success, fear of failure, low self-esteem, codependency, addictions of all sorts, or millions of other issues we focus on to maintain distance from our perceived reality. I am no expert; however, I do have experience, strength, and hope to share. I am just like you. I am on this path of recovery; sometimes rocky, sometimes flat, sometimes painful, and sometimes joyful. And, sometimes, I am just calm and peaceful and comfortable. That is the absolute best; being comfortable in my own skin. Wow, what a concept! I surely wasn't in that place when I started my journey!

So, how did I come up with my title? Well, if you are in recovery, you probably have heard the phrase, "To thine ownself be true." thousands of times. It is even on medallions we are awarded at anniversaries of recovery. But what exactly does that mean? Who am I? What does it mean to be true to myself? Is it just going to meetings, and reading, and talking to others? Or is it more than that? For me, I "got by" for so long, I didn't even recognize that's what I was doing. I just wanted to get through what was happening. I was a passive bystander of my own life. I didn't have an investment. Life happened to me. If you only knew what happened...you would understand. But even I didn't understand. I was just like millions of others who had stopped drinking. And I even stayed "stopped"! I am a "one-chip wonder", which only means I never drank after my last drink. But my life wasn't really all that different. I just busied myself by going to a lot of meetings. I couldn't stand to be alone. I had no idea what I was like; but I knew I didn't like me. After all, I must be worthless if I had done some of the things I had done and had done to me some of the things that were done to me. I had no self-worth, no self-esteem. I only had "other-esteem". This was a new term and concept for me; but once I heard it, I totally knew that was me: What you thought of me was all that was important. I based everything about myself on what *you* thought of me; and how I felt about me wasn't important. I didn't know how to think for myself or not hate myself. I didn't know what I liked; only what you liked. What you thought of me was how I viewed myself. Did I have self-love? You must be kidding... That wasn't possible for me; I was just a composite of labels and broken shards I used to define myself. Between the things that happened to me (sexual, mental, emotional, and spiritual abuse), and what I did to myself, as an alcoholic with a distorted body image; including being a "fat girl" and compulsive overeater, a codependent with sexual identity issues, suicidal ideations, and even more descriptors and pieces of me that evolved came over time. All of my choices and actions were a result of how I related to things or people, but not how I related to *me*. I knew how to survive; not very well, but enough to get by, though painfully. But I didn't know how to do more than that. I certainly didn't know how to be whole or how to thrive.

I know, the word "thrive" is so overused. But I really thing it applies here. Before I got sober and began my recovery journey, I didn't have any tools to get through life without just getting by. Today, I have a life that is full and rich. It still has lots of ups and downs and all-arounds, as that is a part of life (as I now know).What's different is that I don't lose *me* anymore. I'm not wandering around in the weeds looking for who or what **you** want me to be. I use the tools I have learned, and get to the other side, better than I could before! And you can too. But it takes time, patience, and lots of willingness. And others...lots of others. It isn't a loner journey. "WE" is one of the most powerful tools I have discovered. I am no longer alone. I was so lost and alone when I began my journey in 1984. Today, I have many people in my life that truly love me and that I intensely love and care about. We are a part of each other's lives. It is what I always wanted but didn't know how to get. And all I had to give up was everything. And I had to learn new skills and develop new tools. And practice. Repeat. And practice some more. And keep coming back. Never give up. Never let my disease win.

I have had this book in my head for over 20 years. I have tons of reasons why I never got past the title, none of which are very realistic; but then again, not much in recovery does make sense. Everything contained in this book is a part of me. It is a culmination of years of meetings, therapy, self-discovery, and much more. As I said earlier, I am not an expert, just a fellow traveler on this recovery journey. I don't think any of us have all the answers for others, not even for ourselves. That is why recovery is a process...*lots* of trial and error. What works for one, may not work for the other. That said, I am just putting words to paper, and, as we have all heard millions of times; take what you need and leave the rest. Hopefully you will discover some tools that will help you become more comfortable with yourself and learn to thrive instead of just survive!

One of the biggest reasons I didn't start writing this book earlier is that I didn't think I was good enough. I still have areas of my life that are "under construction", and I haven't yet "arrived". I still overeat, have self-esteem issues, can be downright bitchy at times, and am really, *really* human; feelings and all!! I thought I had to be a shining example; and, well, I guess I am. I am no better and no worse than anyone else. And that is what I finally understand is what the journey is all about. I am an active member of the human-race. I am not an observer of life. I am participating in my life on a daily basis. Sometimes I flourish, and sometimes I struggle. It is all a part of the great balancing act we all have to learn to perform.

So, due to having LOTS of time right now, I thought I would finally just get started. I choose to use this time of social distancing and being safer-at-home during the pandemic to explore my creative side; and writing is one of the ways I am taking advantage of during this unexpected opportunity. I lost my job due to COVID-19, and for a while, I lost my identity. I didn't know how to "be" if I wasn't helping someone else. I made several hundred masks and sent to friends and organizations. This was the beginning of my interest in sewing. I have made lots of fun things, which lead to other avenues that led to even more opportunities - which led me to this book. This is yet another way I can give back what was given to me; sometimes freely, sometimes at a cost, as pain was almost always involved. The process of recovery isn't pretty. It is about facing a lot of things I never wanted to face. It was learning to risk, and to trust, and to explore my past and present, as well as prepare for my future. It is filled with joy and fear and is sometimes overwhelming; even the "good" stuff. That is why we don't do it alone. "WE" work together with like-minded people. We share this journey. I am no longer alone. That feeling of being all by myself, with only my fears and tears as companions, is no longer first and foremost in my life. Today, I am loved, and love many people. Today, I know we may all be different, but at our core, we are all the same.

You may be in recovery from an addiction or just the process of living. I think we all have "stuff" we need to work on if we are honest with ourselves. We have a multitude of abilities that can enable us to be the best and truest "self" possible, if we can just be able to look at the dark monster, or monsters, in the closet. I would submit that most of us have a plethora of areas of opportunity to uncover and recover from. I say opportunity; because I can choose to be a victim; or I can choose to become whole. It is up to me. It is work; and sometimes that feels like a four-letter word. Sometimes it is scary; but when we work on our pains, we turn on the lights, and find the monster is just pain hiding from the light of truth and willingness. That can be the most empowering gift we ever give ourselves; but we must do the work. Nothing, absolutely nothing can do it for us, or take away those shards of pain that have fractured our lives and left us fragmented. But, slowly and painstakingly, we can remove the pieces that don't fit and heal from the inside out. Then, and only then, can we become true to ourselves.

I have heard it said, "It's not that I live in the past, but that the past lives on in me." This is very accurate for me; but I now know I no longer have to let my past determine my present or future. The question is, however; how can we take those experiences that hurt so badly and use them to change the future? Well, my best hope is that this book will help you find some tools to help clear out the wreckage of the past and build a strong foundation for a new and full life.

I know this may all seem new and perhaps even scary. The road of recovery is filled with new ideas, new terms, new everything! Addiction is giving up everything for one thing, and recovery is giving up that *one* thing for *everything*. Yes, you **can** do it; one day, one word, one tear, and one laugh at a time!

My Own Definitions and Terms

Here are some terms I will use in this book and what they mean to me. Now that being said, that doesn't mean they are the absolute definitions that Webster or Wikipedia might provide; but they are *my* translation and understanding and what has worked for me. I believe in keeping it simple, but I know in recovery we learn a whole new language. You can always conduct an online search to find other definitions. That is a good practice. Back in the "good old days", we used to keep a dictionary next to our Big Book to look up terms that we had never heard before. Having a dictionary on my phone is so much easier; but sometimes, it just feels good to feel paper and look at a real book.

Disease Concept:

Some people have a problem with the word "disease" being associated with our addiction. I am not here to tell you what is right for you, only what I believe is true for me. It was explained to me long ago that we suffer from a "dis-ease"; I had no ease when I was in my addiction. I had no coping skills, or at least not many, other than resorting to my addiction. This made a lot of sense to me, and I don't have a problem talking or thinking about the disease concept as it relates to my negative behaviors - those "things" that keep me from being true to myself. So, when you see the word disease, just imagine a hyphen between the s and e if it helps - or, just replace it with a word of your choice. There is no wrong or right way to do anything in recovery. We get to learn from everything. Even pain. And joy. My sponsor told me a long time ago that I could take what I need and leave the rest; and that I can always go back for seconds! She also told me that even if I did exactly what she did on her journey, I would not get the same results. This didn't make sense to me for a long time, but now I understand. We start our process of recovery with our *own* baggage; and even though it may look similar, it isn't the same. So, as we begin to unravel the components, and sort through all the pain, we will have different results. My experiences may not be the same as yours, but we all got to this same place just the same. Now, we get to work through all the same obstacles, a step at a time,

Guilt versus Shame:

Guilt is a feeling we experience when we have done or said something wrong that might be viewed as unacceptable. Shame is experienced when we feel we are a "wrong" person at our core because of what we said or did. An easy way to remember it is this way: "I made a mistake versus I *am* a mistake." The goal is to be able to change our way of thinking and internalizing our behavior.

Internalized self-phobia:

Let's break down each word: "internalized" means I turn things in on myself; "self" being pretty easy to understand; and "phobia" is an irrational fear. So, if you put them all together: "Internalized self-phobia" is an irrational fear of who or what I think of me, and/or who or how I feel others perceive me.

Other-esteem versus Self-esteem

"Other-esteem" is looking *outside* of myself for validation, direction, and/or a sense of identity. "Self-esteem" is the ability to look *inside* myself for validation, self-direction, and a healthy identity. Are you and "innee" or an"outee"?

Sponsor:

A sponsor is simply someone who has worked the steps of recovery and can share their experiences, strength, encouragement, and hope with you. They aren't our parents, financial advisors, therapists, lawyers, or anything else. Though they may be that in their professions or other roles, that is NOT why they serve as sponsors; and that is not how they are to be utilized.

Feelings Dictionary:

A feelings dictionary is an individualized and very personal understanding of what each feeling looks and feels like as you encounter them; how that emotion expresses itself and is manifested in your body. It also encompasses the thoughts that are attached to the experiences; thereby assisting you in understanding and becoming comfortable with each emotion, as well as how you relate and react to them.

Just know that though there may be words or phrases that are unfamiliar to you, you will develop your own/personal understanding, as time goes by. I might suggest you start a dictionary of your own, with new terms and phrases you hear in meetings, that you don't understand yet; so that as you discover your "definition" and understanding, you can create your own personal dictionary.

The most important thing is to just **keep coming back**!! As we hear in meetings, more will be discovered and revealed as we progress!

Chapter One

Manage versus Recover

"My mission in life is not merely to survive, but to thrive; and to do so with some passion, some compassion, some humor, and some style." - Maya Angelou

"Manage, to get by." is a phrase I am all too familiar with. If we are honest with ourselves, we may all recall having spoken something like this phrase, or at least hearing someone else say it. But, just as the old song asks, "Is that all there is?" we all at times felt hopeless and found ourselves in a survival-mode; just striving to survive. That song brings back so many memories. Yikes! I see myself, a lonely teenager, lying on my bed listening to Peggy Lee singing and just...wanting...to...die; or at least to stop all my horrible feelings of self-hatred and self-doubt and fear; but not knowing how - feeling that I was all alone in the world, and nobody could possibly understand what I was thinking and feeling. Teenage angst is so pervasive and inescapable; at least for me it was. I can't remember a time when I was growing up that I didn't just "get by". I made decent grades in high school, without studying. I got through college, with a BA degree! (I refer to this as my "Bachelors of Alcoholism"!) I never had any self-discipline. That is still a struggle of mine, except for staying sober. In early recovery I was terrified of going back out and losing myself again to my disease. Within my first few years of sobriety, I had begun my inner-child recovery work, and made a life I never knew I could have: I had friends that truly cared for me and loved me unconditionally. I had a career that allowed me to make a difference in peoples' lives. I had a little money in the bank; and most importantly, I had started liking myself, (or at least not hating myself so much). That was when I first realized the difference between "managing" and "recovering". And it began with looking at things inside of me that were painful and scary. But none of it did I do alone. I went to therapists and meetings and worked the steps and did inventories and kept trudging on every day - one day at a time. After a while, I didn't feel like I was a stranger to myself anymore. I became able to actually be quiet, be alone with myself, and not have to "do" anything. I no longer was bouncing my leg anytime I sat for more than a few seconds, because I couldn't sit still longer than that. I stopped feeling like I had to run away; my fight, flight or freeze buttons weren't always exposed and ready to be pushed by anyone, anywhere. I started being able to see a bigger picture and even make plans for the future. I used to hate it when people would ask me what my five-year-plan for the future was: hell, I just wanted to get through the day! How was I supposed to know what five years from now looks like? Truthfully, I wasn't even sure I wanted to live that long.

Today, I have a five-year plan: Retirement. Travel. Enjoying life. Finishing writing this book! And so much more. Today, I know I can, and will continue to explore, have adventures, and *thrive*!

One of the misconceptions is that people get into recovery because they "have to". However, recovery isn't for those who "need" it, but for those who "want" it. If everyone who "needed" to get sober or change their addictive behaviors recognized and responded to that "need"; there would be recovery centers on every corner, working 24/7, and a long line of people out the door waiting to get inside. That isn't the case, as we all know. It is not a fast "cure-all", or even a guarantee that if you do everything "just right", you will become perfect. That's just never going to happen. It is a life-long process and journey. It is also messy and takes an enormous level of commitment to do the work. Sometimes we can see and feel our progress, and sometimes we can't; *but* we have to just keep on keepin' on! It will get better; but first, it gets really different!

So, how do we make the shift from "manage" to "recover"? Well, hopefully that is what this book will help you with. Now, don't think you have to do everything the way I did it, or that this book will tell you everything you need to know about your own recovery. I am sharing what has worked for me and for the many other people I have learned from; but this is by no means "THE" answer to how to get into and stay in recovery from whatever your destructive patterns were. But it is a good start; and we have to start the journey somewhere if we want to be different! If nothing changes, nothing changes. Now, let's

To Thine Own Self Be True

get going!!

Chapter 2

Surrender, Dorothy!

"We must be willing to let go of the life we have planned, so as to have the life that is waiting for us." - Joseph Campbell

Give up? Are you crazy? I would lose everything! I can't afford to lose! That would make me a loser; and I already feel like one! What do you mean surrender?

I know this sounds very counter-intuitive; but in reality, it is actually an essential component of making forward progress. Sometimes we need to stop, reassess where we are and where we want to go, in order to reach our ultimate destination.

In the process of recovery, there are times when we have to realize that fighting and resisting what is causing us distress is unnecessary. We have to drop the bat and stop hitting ourselves over the head with it before we can realize there might just be another way of doing things. That is what this adventure we are on is all about: developing new tools and learning how to use them the way they are meant to be used. This reminds me of an example of an improper use of a tool: I was walking on our deck and a nail was sticking up. Rather than go inside and get a hammer, I saw a screwdriver lying on the table. So, I picked it up and started hammering the nail with the end of the screwdriver. Not only did it not hammer in the nail, it broke the handle of the screwdriver. Now I had to buy a new screwdriver! And I still had to go inside and get the hammer! Not using the right tool for the job is not the most effective way to work. The same applies to our recovery. Surrender, not giving in or giving up, is sometimes an integral part of the solution; and learning when to let go is just as important to how to let go.

Sometimes, I have to remind myself, "Would I rather be right, or would I rather be happy?" Of course, I always want to be right, but at what cost? And is being "right" going to make everything better? This all reflects my levels of self-esteem. Just admitting I am wrong does not make me a bad person. I am only human. That is one thing I hate sometimes. It is taking the good with the bad that is hard sometimes. This is especially true when it comes to emotions. And, in reality, there isn't a "good" or "bad" emotion. They just *are* - an integral part of our make-up. Eliminating judgmental words is another important tool in my toolbox; words like, "good", "bad", "wrong", and "right" and even "positive" and "negative" can all be prejudicial in nature. Using words like "healthy" and "unhealthy" are less critical to our core-being. By eliminating this judgmental language from our vocabulary, we are learning to be self-affirming, and are moving toward becoming our own best friend - which is a huge part of surrendering.

There are definitely times and situations when it is in your best interest to stand up for yourself. However, it is also important to look at what the consequences of doing that might be. There are consequences to everything we do; sometimes they are easy to overcome, sometimes difficult. Just be sure you aren't reacting out of shame or pain, but, instead out of a clear understanding that you are facing the event the best way you can *today,* and using the tools of recovery you have learned so far. Know that life is messy; that we all make mistakes because we are human, and not because we are bad or doing it the wrong way. We get the gift of learning from everything. Today I just want to limit my painful learning experiences as much as I can. Also, I try not to have to make amends for my behaviors or my responses. When I do make amends, it isn't just saying, "I'm sorry"; then repeating the behavior Amends are about mending our behavior; making the changes necessary to be the healthiest person I can be at the time. It is progress, not perfection! And, I have found that peace is far more precious than perfection. Choosing to be *in recovery*, rather than doing what I have always done, or what I think is expected of me, is old behavior. It doesn't bring me to the person I want to become. It also isn't easy. In fact, it is often down-right uncomfortable. However, each time I *respond* rather than *react*, I get the opportunity to experience a healthier, more positive outcome!

Old behaviors, old tapes, old belief systems are just that: OLD. They don't "fit" the person that lives in the present. And, when we discover what the old messages that have determined our behaviors and experiences;

then make decisions to change them, we get to have more opportunities for growth.

It is important to remember that recovery is not about blaming others for our past; it is about learning to accept personal responsibility for all our decisions and progressing on a *new* path. With all change, pain is an inevitable part of the process and the journey; but it will not be more than we can endure. Most importantly it isn't the end of the journey, but a new beginning! We have already lived through and survived the challenges and difficulties; now we are learning to process and respond to them in a healthy, constructive way.

We may need assistance with this. It is not a sign of weakness to ask for help. Actually, the exact opposite is true, as it shows your willingness to be different, to choose a different reality and future. You may choose to go to therapy, or perhaps utilize a sponsor or mentor that understands and can guide and support you in the process you are undertaking. Whatever you decide, just make sure you feel safe.

What do I mean by old tapes or old behaviors? They are the often-repeated messages we heard while growing up, that don't work for us. Where they came from isn't as important as what we do with them. They may have originated from our family of origin, society, television, movies, news, friends, acquaintances, or anywhere. Oftentimes, they were unwritten rules that were expectations or habits that were ultimately self-defeating.

What are some of the old tapes or messages that are preventing you from being true to yourself? We will learn more about the practice of inventory, and how to change old thinking into healthy self-talk in coming chapters.

Chapter 3

Don't let your hang-ups trip you up

"What you live with you learn, what you learn you practice, what you practice you become, what you become has consequences." - Earnie Larsen

Hurtful habits are hang-ups; prejudices; pre-conceived notions; fears. All of these are impediments that prevent you from becoming the best friend to yourself and others than you can be. It is the wedge that is placed between you and others that separates you from your real self. It is what is comfortably familiar, even though it is also painful.

"HOW" to be different, you might ask? By using the H.O.W. acronym of Honesty, Open-mindedness, and Willingness to examine your beliefs; so that you can determine if they fit who you are today and where you want to go. Just because your family always did it "this way", or you have always done it "that way" doesn't mean it actually works for you or is a fit for your life today.

I remember a story that Melody Beattie shared about cutting off the end of the ham for a holiday meal. She finally asked why her family always did that and, in doing so, learned that it was because her grandma's pan was too small for the ham! We do this with so many things! We continue repeating the same actions, not because they make sense, but because they are familiar – we've always "done it that way!"

As a child, I was very inquisitive. I was always asking, "Why?" I know I got on my family's nerves often! I seemed to always need to know the answers; but it seemed there were never any to be found. Eventually, I learned not to question why, because no one was going to answer. I didn't feel anybody really cared anyway; or, at least, that was the impression I got. Many children of abusive or neglectful families were punished or dismissed for asking; so, we learned, for one reason or another, not to ask.

In college, on the first day of one of my classes my professor said the most amazing thing. He said, "Question everything." Such heresy! How can we do that??? That conflicted with everything I knew or had ever been told! But in reality, that is exactly what we have to do in order to make the changes that are necessary for our growth.

"If we always do what we've always done, we will always get what we always got." That is a saying I have heard for so long, with no idea where it came from. I know it is true for me, though. I have to be willing to change; to be uncomfortable, in order to become my best self.

Habits are just repeated patterns of behavior. It is humorously said that if we do something twice, it becomes a habit, whether it is good for us or not. I think there is a lot of truth to that. "Repetition strengthens and confirms.", so the saying goes. The more I do something, the more I will continue to do it. The same principle can be applied to our recovery. In order to make a change, we have to take action - even if it doesn't feel right. Actually, it *won't* feel right at first. That's the point! It's called "growing pains" for a reason. I don't have to like it; but if I want to be different and have a different outcome, I have to do what it takes to change. It isn't easy, but it is really basic: *just do it*!

As the quote at the beginning of the chapter stated, we become what we live with and practice; therefore the consequence is we become healthier people in recovery.

So, let's look at some of the things that have hung you out to dry, or kept you from fulfilling your dreams. What areas are causing you discomfort because they aren't working anymore? Look at your daily routine. Are there areas for improvement, such as your morning practice? Could you possibly start the day with reading from a meditation book? Or, maybe add a reading from a recovery book, even if it's only a few paragraphs. You don't have to read the whole book. Little changes will create the space for bigger changes. How about ending the day with a gratitude list? One of my favorites is an alphabetical list. "B" is always easy for me. (Thanks, Ben B. for introducing this awesome tool to me!) Another is to list 10 ways you participated in your recovery that day. Just be sure that whatever you decide to include is related to how you made positive changes that can help you to see you are becoming a healthier person.

Do you find that you have certain behaviors you feel you can't change? Try this challenge: brush your teeth and your hair with your non-dominant hand. It may be difficult at first, or at the very least funny! I remember when I had carpal tunnel syndrome and had to use my left hand for everything. It was so hard initially; but then I became a whiz, especially in changing gears when driving my manual transmission car! Hey; I had to get around, so I learned to do what I needed to do.

In our disease, we may exhibit character traits that aren't exactly healthy; but if we can learn to redirect them in a positive way, we can change our outcome. In 12-step vernacular this is often referred to as character defects. Now, let's look at this in depth. First of all, this does not mean you are defective just because you have unhealthy character traits or have used them in a way that isn't productive. All it means is that you have often used your healthy character traits in a negative manner or to excess. There is nothing abnormal about this. Actually, it is very human. We just need to become aware of the ways in which we are using our positive/healthy traits as weapons instead of as tools.

An example of turning a negative trait into a positive one is procrastination. In my disease, it can lead me to doing nothing, which leads to feelings of shame, because doing nothing results in creating more pain and chaos around me. In my recovery, however, I can use it to put off taking the first drink. It is all about learning how to use our tools productively and appropriately, as opposed to turning them inward and beating ourselves up.

Let's see what dictionary.com has to say so we can further understand this concept:

Defect [noun dee-fekt, dih-fekt] [i]

1. *a shortcoming, fault, or imperfection: a defect in an argument; a defect in a machine.*
2. *lack or want, especially of something essential to perfection or completeness; deficiency: a defect in hearing.*

Character [noun kar-ik-ter] ii

1. *the aggregate of features and traits that form the individual nature of some person or thing: one such feature or trait; characteristic.*
2. *moral or ethical quality: a man of fine, honorable character.*

So, when we look at the definitions above and combine them, we actually see that character defects are shortcomings or imperfections that combine to create traits that form an individual.

We can be bound by our habits; not knowing or understanding their source or how to do "it" differently. But learning what they are will give us insight into how to make the necessary changes to change a "negative" outcome into a "positive" outcome.

Always remember: *more will be revealed!*

Chapter 4

Boundaries versus Walls

"Setting boundaries is a way of caring for myself. It doesn't make me mean, selfish, or uncaring (just) because I don't do things your way. I care about me, too." - Christine Morgan

Knowing what is keeping us separate from others or what we want to be is crucial to our new journey. But before we can just willy-nilly start changing things, let's take an objective look at the information needed before we leap into the process. First, we need to evaluate what is keeping us safe, what is holding us hostage and the difference between the two. That is where we determine whether we have set up boundaries or walls.

What is the difference between a boundary and a wall? Why do we have them? Why do we need to know what they are? What do they look like? Why, why, why??? All three are excellent questions. Let's look at the definitions given by dictionary.com, as well as some synonyms:

Boundary [boun-duh-ree, -dree] [iii]
- *something that indicates bounds or limits; a limiting or bounding line.*
- *also called frontier.*

Some synonyms of the word boundary are:

barrier	frontier
border	horizon
bounds	line
confines	perimeter
edge	

Wall [wawl] [iv]

- any of various permanent upright constructions having a length much greater than the thickness and presenting a continuous surface except where pierced by doors, windows, etc.: used for shelter, protection, or privacy, or to subdivide interior space, to support floors, roofs, or the like, to retain earth, to fence in an area, etc.
- usually walls. a rampart raised for defensive purposes.

Some synonyms for wall are:

Barricade	Screen
Block	Side
blockade	Limitation
Dam	Restriction
Embankment	Roadblock
Fence	Stockade

All of the above information being considered, the best way I can define a boundary is that it is a healthy separation between me and others. It is when I am able to stay on my side of the street and not be "messing in other people's business". I am not controlling or judging. I am a part of, but not in control of, the relationship or the situation. It is simply when I recognize where I "end" and the other person starts. It is an unimpaired position that allows me to have my beliefs and values, but not have to convert your views to mine, or give my well-being to you. It is not a wall that keeps me from seeing you or your viewpoint, but only a distance wherein we are not enmeshed.

"Separate but equal" is a good way to think of this. I have my beliefs, opinions, views, etc., and you have yours. Neither is better or worse, just different. Both of us are capable of keeping our identities intact. Boy that sounds like Utopia doesn't it? It *is* possible, however. Maybe not constantly, but we can progress toward achieving this goal more and more over time. And with lots of practice.

First, we have to know what our beliefs and values are and take a hard look at our expectations. What is important to me? Do I need to be right all the time? Do I need to control every situation? Is what you think of me more important than what I think of me? If I revisit the definitions above, a couple of words stand out to me. The word "frontier" for boundary makes me think of being an explorer; which is what we are during recovery; and the word "defensive" for wall brings to mind being fearful that we will be overtaken or being always on guard, which is what we are before we begin our recovery. Also, it points out that "wall" is a permanent structure. It doesn't have to stay that way, however! We can break it down, one stone at a time. But we have to recognize and acknowledge that it *is* there, as well as what each stone represents in our wall.

I believe it is just a structure created by and consisting of pain: some resulting from small "hurts" and some from large blows. All of them are created from injury to the core of our being. And we have to grieve each and every one of these injuries. It is a slow process; but the inventory process is essential to uncovering the root of the pain - discovering the components that are needed to work through the events; then recovery is the natural by-product of the work done on and with each stone in the wall. It is not a "one and done" process. It takes time and patience and work. It is also important to remind yourself that it is a journey not a destination. And some of the bigger stones will take longer to remove than the smaller stones. But with work the burden becomes less; and you become less trapped by your past and can enjoy the present more and more. We will discuss the grief process and tools for processing grief in a later chapter.

So, how do we catalog our pains? Let's look at the "how" we can learn ways to use the inventory tool, as well as some other writing tools.

Chapter 5

The "Write" Stuff

"The secret of getting ahead is getting started." - Mark Twain

One of the most important tools of my recovery has been writing. I haven't always liked it; in fact, sometimes I have downright hated it. Well, maybe, if I am to be really honest, it isn't that I hated it as much as I was afraid of it – or at least what writing might bring up from the depths of my chaos and pain. The first "big" thing I had to write was my 4th step inventory. It terrified me. There were things I had long since determined I would take to my grave. "No one is going to know that about me," was my guiding principle. And it almost destroyed me. I kept hearing that in recovery we are "as sick as our secrets"; and I definitely had secrets. At least secrets I kept close at hand; ready to use against me at any moment. No, I didn't kill anyone or rob a bank or any of the million other things that I believed were what people thought would constitute "bad". No, my "secrets" had to do with things that had happened to me (with and without my consent), thoughts about myself, and things I didn't do instead of things I did.

There are many ways to introduce writing into your recovery. Journaling is a great way to get started. The process of pen to paper (or fingers to keyboard) begins building body memories that allows you to start getting comfortable with putting words down. I have found that by writing by hand (rather than typing on a keyboard) allows me to connect physically to the information, therefore get into the core of my feelings more easily. Then, there is also the ritual of finding just the "right" pen and paper. Sometimes I like to use different colors of ink pens depending on my mood; purple is my favorite, but if I am really into anger, I want RED!

For me journaling helps me process the day's events, or gain an understanding of something that has caused me to feel uncomfortable and find out what it might really be about. You can journal daily, weekly, or just sporadically. That is what I do now more than I did initially.

Another resource is list-making. A word of caution, however: don't get hung up on completing the list; it is just a guide, not a master. Making lists of things I want to accomplish, or even better, a list of what I have accomplished is a good practice to get into! One of my sponsors gave me a great tool to use at the end of the day: List 10 ways I participated in my recovery today. It isn't as easy as it sounds; especially when you are in a funky mood.

The inventory process is incredibly healing. It is where I learned the difference between placing blame and assigning responsibility. It isn't just making a list and checking it twice, though. There isn't any magic involved, just willingness to work through the pain in order to get to the other side. But, it isn't something we need to automatically know how to do; our sponsor will guide us through this process.

But writing, in and of itself, isn't the whole

package. It has to be a combination of writing and sharing. And the sharing must be with someone you trust. I have heard it said in meetings that "open 5ths (inventory) lead to open fifths (booze)". I understand that. To me it means that it may not be in my best interest to just share anything and everything openly with anyone or everyone, and definitely not intimate details in a meeting! That degree of sharing is to be done with your sponsor and/or therapist! It is about learning to have healthy boundaries and how to share appropriately. It is also about trust and risk. It is about building relationships based in recovery, not hearsay or drama.

When I became willing to trade my shame for recovery, my life was changed forever. Now, let's be honest: the first inventory I shared with my sponsor was not thorough. I picked and chose what I would share; thinking that it would be enough to keep me sober, as well as still have her think "good" of me. But that didn't last long. Once Sandora's box was opened and the lid off, nothing was going to shut it again. The shame that was still inside me poisoned my thoughts and kept me separate from my friends and recovery family. I had to get honest. For ME this time, not for anyone else. So, I wrote everything I hadn't shared before and took it to my sponsor to read. I could not say it out loud. It was too painful, too shameful. So, the best I could do was to throw the spiral notebook at her and tell her to read it as I ran out of the room. Now, I don't suggest anyone else ever throw anything at anyone, but it was the best I could do then. I had to get rid of all of that crap. And I knew I couldn't say it out loud.

After she read it, she came to me and said, "Oh, my god...", and my heart stopped. I knew in that single instant all my fears were confirmed; that she hated me, that I was as worthless as I knew I was, that, even in recovery there was no place for me. Then she finished her sentence: "We are just alike." WOW! I couldn't believe it! She didn't hate me. All the chatter between my ears all those years had just been my disease lying to me, filling me with self-hate so I would continue drowning in my self-defeating, self-loathing behaviors. She went on to relate that the facts weren't the same, but the feelings were. That is when she shared with me, "We have a feelings disease; therefore, we have to have a feelings recovery." I still remember it as though it was yesterday. It was the very first time I truly felt I fit in anywhere. I had found my people. Also, even more importantly, I had found ME; or, at least, the beginning of ME.

Another form of inventory is the "spot-check inventory". The spot-check inventory is one that is really important to utilize, to help us get a take on what is going on inside ourselves. We can use this tool whenever we have a gut reaction to something. It allows us to start understanding our feelings-dictionary and what past garbage is attached to present events. We don't have to write this method unless it will help us get to the bottom of what's going on.

There are a couple of phrases that I learned when getting comfortable with writing that are still important to me. The first is, "Name it; claim it; dump it." I use this method often, especially when I am trying to figure out what is causing some restlessness, irritability, or emotional discomfort. I think about when I started feeling funky, then recall a time when I felt this way before. Usually, this takes some time and exploring, but once I find the root of it all, I can let it go. Now, I may have to write more than once on a subject before I get it resolved, but it does happen; and because I have been honest in my appraisal, it is an incredible relief. And if it resurfaces again, I can just "name it, claim it, and dump it" again.

The second phrase is similar to the first. It is "Uncover. Discover. Recover." Again, it is about taking account of a part of my life that I am ready to be free from and looking at how it is manifesting itself in my present life; then I can make the changes necessary to remove its presence and know I have come to a much better understanding of myself and my journey. Uncover the past, discover how it is affecting me today, and make the changes necessary for my recovery. Simple, but not easy! And it takes time and practice.

Yes, I know; it can be very challenging to get to the crux of what we are experiencing. One of the most powerful ways of realizing there is something from the past inflicting pain on the present, is that when you have an intense reaction to any event, it probably isn't about that situation or experience. It most likely is attached to a pain from the past. So, by using the spot-check inventory, we can acknowledge there may be something to look at, and maybe even later do a more detailed inventory. For now, though, you can just acknowledge there is something to work on, breathe, get grounded, and move on.

What do I mean by the word "grounded"? Sometimes I feel as though I am off- kilter and may be feeling anxiety or some other emotion I can't recognize but is still causing me distress. By using a simple technique, I can get out of that panic and in touch with reality and be able to go on with my day. It may take more than one effort to get there initially, but eventually and with practice, it becomes much easier to achieve calm.

Here are a couple techniques I have learned that help me become grounded:

1.   Put your middle finger and thumb together and take a deep breath in through your nose, hold it for a few seconds, then exhale through your mouth. If you can close your eyes and imagine a safe place, do that. But sometimes it isn't wise to close your eyes!

So, just do what you can at the moment. Repeat to yourself an affirmation or just remind yourself that it came to "pass", not to stay. After a few breaths, you should feel more grounded. It will take time to build the body memories, but eventually you will find (or at least I did) that just the process of joining the digits together brings relief.

2. Another method of grounding is mindfulness. There are many ways to practice mindfulness. Here are my two favorites:

a. Focus on something right in front of you. When I first got sober, I smoked. My sponsor would tell me that when I was feeling overwhelmed to focus on the tip of my cigarette, watch the red glow, the smoke float gently in the air, and breathe naturally. Anything that brings you into the hear-and-now is what you are striving to accomplish. It might be a fly on a wall, or a zit on someone's face; whatever we can focus on to get us out of the anxiety of the moment. Just remember to breathe naturally, and repeat to yourself that all is ok, and that you can and will get through this.

b. Another way is the 5-4-3-2-1 system.

Take a deep breath, and then focus on each of your senses. First, list 5 things you see; then 4 things you feel (like the wind on your face, etc.); then 3 things you hear; then 2 things you smell; and lastly, 1 thing you taste. If you can't remember which sense comes in what order, it doesn't really matter. Just focus on your senses. Focusing on your senses forces you to be present in the moment and reduces the fear and anxiety that can be attached to old or unresolved experiences.

You may find other ways of becoming present, and that is why we are always changing, always growing, always working to better ourselves and get to know ourselves better. That's what recovery is all about.

▯

Chapter 6

Feelings, whoa oh Oh Crap!

"I'm a human being having human emotions. I don't like it." - Anonymous BB

My sponsor told me early on: "We have a feelings disease therefore we have to have a feelings recovery." I had no idea what she was talking about then. She might as well have been speaking to me in Portuguese. I was clueless as to what I really felt. I thought I knew, but upon closer inspection, I really was at a loss. It took me quite some time to get to know my own feelings dictionary. When I first got sober, I thought I "might" have some anger issues. What I realized was I went from zero to rage instantly, and really didn't know what anger was, or what it felt like. I knew to stuff my anger down deep; because you weren't allowed to be angry. In my family, my father had a bad heart, and it was an unspoken rule (and sometimes spoken) that you never shared your anger near him; it might cause him to have a heart attack. And he had lots of them. So, I came to believe that "I" caused him to have heart attacks; because I was a kid and didn't really know how to keep my feelings to myself. When he died, I was 14; and I inwardly knew I had done that to him. Hogwash. He had a bad heart. It wasn't my fault. I am not that powerful. But I didn't know that then, and I certainly didn't have anyone explain that to me. It took several years in recovery to finally understand, accept this reality, and be able to let it go.

I thought feelings were bad, and that I "shouldn't" have them. So, I tried, with all my heart, to be the good little girl and not have feelings - any feelings. But, since I have always been an empath, I feel everything deeply. I remember coming home from high school so many times upset because somebody did or said something that hurt my feelings. I would be crying and wanting to die - like that would take care of *that*. Teenage anguish is so painful. I don't know how we get through it, (and some of us don't). But, on one particular day, my mom came into my room and asked me what was wrong. I told her something, I don't remember what, but what she said was the stupidest thing I had ever heard. She said, "You have to feel pain if you are ever going to feel joy." How insensitive of her. I thought she was the worst mother ever, and how could she say that? Didn't she know how bad I hurt? A few years later I realized she was the smartest woman I knew. She was much smarter than I was. She knew that all feelings are important, and that if we deny one, we deny them all. Getting acquainted with our emotions isn't easy, and in the beginning we only understand a few surface feelings. The most common feelings are fear, anger, sad, and happy. I have come to learn that when I feel angry, it isn't always anger. For me, it is usually fear based. So, I have to look deeper to see what is really going on; what am I afraid of? Usually, it is the fear that I won't get what I want, or I will lose something I have. And this goes for all our emotions; we have to learn our own feelings dictionary. I have to have a physical sensation connected to an emotion for me to really understand what it is that I am experiencing.

Another good example is love. How many times did I fall in love? If I look at it more closely, wasn't it just lust? Or maybe even just loneliness? I only know that in order for me to really be present in the moment, I must be aware of what is real, instead of what I "think" I am feeling.

Oh, and don't even get me started on sad. I totally didn't know how to grieve appropriately. I was at a total loss; I knew despondency and depression, but I had no way to actually just feel sad. I seemed to always go to extremes. But the key was time and learning what I was feeling at the same time I was feeling it. One of my sponsors gave me an amazing tool that is still an important one in my toolbox: whenever I am experiencing a more intense reaction than the event calls for, it is probably about something else; likely connected to the past. And, until I can learn to identify what is going on, I will stay stuck in old behaviors and old feelings.

As discussed earlier, one of the ways we learn how to decipher our feelings is by using the spot-check inventory. This allows you to just pause, breathe, and look at what is going on around you. Then, you can choose what you do with your feelings; either act on them, or not. What is going to be in your best interest? Sometimes a good thing to ask yourself is this: would you rather be right, or would you rather be happy. Also, ask yourself these 3 questions: 1. Does it need to be said? 2. Does it need to be said by me? 3. Is it kind?

Learning our own feelings dictionary takes time and work. And ours may not look like someone else's expression of feelings. We cannot match our insides with anyone else's outside. Though someone else may they appear to be dealing with a situation better than you, it is possible that they are just dealing with it *different* than you. So, don't set yourself up by feeling that person is better than you, or they are farther along in their recovery than you. That is an unrealistic expectation; and I have heard that "expectations" are just premeditated resentments! That has definitely been proven to be true for me!

In my second year of sobriety, I started

working in a group therapy setting. But before I could attend the first session, there were several assessments I had to complete so the therapist would have a better understanding of where I was in terms of my recovery and what areas needed work. One of the assessments was a feelings inventory. I can't remember how many questions and situations there were, but it seemed to go on forever. After I was finished and she had scored the assessment, she shared with me the results. I scored off the charts in SAD, and very high in RAGE. I had no idea. I just thought I was depressed and maybe a *little* angry. It was very hard to comprehend how I could rate so high on feelings I didn't even know I had! But this was the beginning of me learning my own language and identifying what I was feeling, when I was actually experiencing feelings. It isn't easy, but it has been amazingly worth it in the long run.

Today, most days, I know what I am feeling

when I am feeling. The distance between the event and understanding where I am in my feelings is much shorter than ever and continues to become even sorter, the longer I continue my recovery. Conversely, the longer I am in recovery, the more time I have to react to a situation. I heard a speaker one time share that for every year of sobriety or recovery we experience, we have one more second of response time to a situation. So, in year one, I had one second to respond to a situation. Usually that would be a totally inappropriate response and off-the-cuff. But, today, at 37 years of sobriety I have 37 seconds to reflect and see how I want to respond, and check my emotions and see where I am. Now, that doesn't mean I don't say or do the same stupid thing, but at least I have more time to think it over before I react!

Something else to note about feelings: how do we refer to them? Do we say, "I am angry?" or, "I am sad (or happy or glad or whatever)?" When we say we are something, I think we actually become that thing. So, if you say you angry, that is what you will become. But, if you say, "I feel angry", then it is only a feeling, not a state of being. Try it. See how it feels in your body. Also, look at your fists. Are they clinched? Are you wearing your shoulders for earrings? Your body responds to what you tell it. For me, the difference is very marked, and I can now let go of my attachment to the feelings much faster when they are not a part of who I am, or how I see myself. Another reminder of what we practice, we become; and I didn't get sober to be an angry, miserable person!

This is just a thought. Again, if this doesn't work for you, don't use it. Not all tools are right for everyone. But for me, this was a really important way to distance my relationship with how I respond to my emotions.

Chapter 7

Good Grief

"The only cure for grief is action." - *George Henry Lewes*

One of the most central, and often times untreated, parts of our lives is grief. I really believe that many of us enter recovery, start working the steps on our addiction or self-defeating behavior, but never revisit all the grief that has built up inside. I also believe that if we don't work through our grief, we will continue to find unhealthy ways of coping, and even if we don't revert to our primary addiction, we will not be whole and complete within ourselves.

Learning how to recognize grief and how to

process it appropriately is necessary if we are to find lasting peace and comfort. I bet you thought you only grieved the "big deals" in life - death, divorce, failures, etc. That isn't true. We have to grieve **every** change, positive and negative. Everything is connected and affects how we travel through life, which in turn affects our recovery, or our disease. We have the privilege of choosing how we allow it to impact our lives today. Grief is a stressor; it is often attached to a huge rolled up ball of past hurts and pains. That is why learning to grieve is so critical for our recovery.

Elisabeth Kubler-Ross taught us there are 5 stages of grief: Denial, Anger, Bargaining, Depression, and Acceptance. I always hear this in my head as, "Yabba DABDA do". It helps me to remember all five and evaluate where I am, so I don't miss one. I don't really think we move through these stages in order each time, or maybe it is just that I go through a stage so fast I don't realize it. It depends on the intensity of the grief event. For something small, like misplacing a paper that is due in a class I am taking may only take a few minutes to process, whereas a sickness may take much longer to grieve. This is especially true if there is a big change in my life as a result of the illness.

Grief is a core issue to undertake; it is a process, not an event. And, it is about going *through* it, not just coping *with it*. We have to untangle all the threads of pain and loss and disconnect them from each other. They are synergistic in the approach to survival: the more they stay together, the stronger they are; therefore, the harder to work through separately. It's like a bowl of spaghetti; and recovery is separating each noodle from the others. One strand at a time!

And it takes time and effort to work through each of them. Remember that grief is not linear; it doesn't go in a straight line. Don't think that just because you have worked through one loss it won't come back up again. The grief recovery process is fluid, which means it is constantly changing depending on how much we can tolerate and how deeply we dive in our journey. And don't assume that just because you have "dealt" with a trauma that it changes the past; we cannot change the past. What we can do is alter the effect it has on our life today and in the future. And thus, not be in bondage to the past. We still hurt, especially for the loss of loved ones, lost ideals, etc., because that is life. We aren't above human experience; we learn to embrace our humanness, warts (pain) and all.

So, how do we learn what-all is stock-piled in our grief stash? Some causes will be easy to spot, especially the big losses: death of friends and family. Challenge yourself to look beyond people; however. What about dreams, ambitions, changes in relationships (divorce, break-ups, moves, etc.), job/career changes, physical changes due to sickness, injury, or "just" the aging process. (I say "just" because this is something I am dealing with in my life; and it sucks. I never really had anyone to age around me growing up; so, I don't know what is "normal" or what is not. "Arther Itis" is an asshole; just sayin'!)

Also, don't think that we "only" grieve painful experiences. Grief is our bodies' response to change; positive and negative, joyful and painful. So, when you are looking at your life, be sure that encompasses your entire life, not just the pain. An example of a positive event I had to grieve was when I got a promotion at work. I know that "should" only be a happy experience, but I had to grieve the change in how I related to others at work. No longer was I just one of the gang; now I was their manager, and some of them didn't feel as though they could treat me the same. I had to grieve the change in our relationships and help them see that, even though I had more responsibilities, I was still the same person, and they could come to me and still be my friends. It was a painful and yet exciting time for all of us; but it took time to get to the "comfort zone".

Make a list of the losses and changes in your life. Start with the big ones, and then proceed to the smaller, yet still impactful ones.

Here are *some* possible opportunities to look at:

Moving: (whether as a child or as adult), especially if you had to do this often
Death of a loved one, including pets
Marriage: (you and/or your kids)
Divorce: (you and/or your kids)
Job and/or career changes: (losses or positive adjustments)
Sickness: injury, health changes (even positive ones; and yes, aging is a health change!)

Also, be sure to look closely at any changes in loved ones' health and/or abilities. We are affected by everything around us. So, take the above list and apply it to close family and friends. You will probably discover more opportunities are waiting for you, from which to heal. AND, if we don't address them, they certainly will address us - usually upside the head!

Just look at anything that brings up some form of feelings as you think of them. Write them down. Next, determine where you are on the DABDA list. Are you angry? Do you feel like "things will get better when..." (aka bargaining)? Have you worked through the situation, and are on the other side? It is important to list these feelings as well, so that you can see the progress you have made, and what still needs to be addressed. Remember, this is a LONG-TERM PROCESS! You aren't going to "get over it" in a minute, or even by just writing it down. It takes time and the willingness to let them go. But even as we let them go, they will always be a part of us. We are the sum of all our experiences, and we learn from everything. Also, we are *all* connected.

Chapter 8

Stop should-ing on yourself

"A person who never made a mistake never tried anything new." - Albert Einstein

Shame. Wow. That word is so powerful and permeating. It is one of the tools (or, is the word weapons more appropriate?) of our disease. It is capable of keeping us stuck and questioning everything we learn in recovery. It seems to have a life of its' own. It definitely is a power greater than me....at least until I learn tools to recognize it and make it right sized, so that I can eventually destroy it; one shameful thought, event, feeling, old-tape at a time. One of the ways I have learned to recognize shame is the word "should". Often times, "shoulds" are just old messages that tell us we are doing it "wrong". When I hear that word today, I evaluate if what I am talking about is based in today, or from someone else in the past. An example of this is: "I should know what I want to be when I grow up, but I don't." This is really saying to me that I am not where I want to be. But is that based on my understanding of my life, or is it that what I hear some unknown, unheard voice from the past? Another example is, "I shouldn't do.... (fill in the blank)." Why not? Who told me I couldn't do that? Why do I base my personal beliefs on what others think of me?

One of the most powerful tools to combat shame is when I recognize I am feeling shame, to actually say, "STOP". Now, I may not say this out loud, but sometimes it is the only way I can truly stop the shame spiral. What is a shame spiral? Well, it's the process our emotions take when we experience shame. It is a downward spiral of self doubt, self hatred, internalized anger (aka depression), self loathing, fear, rage, and just overall yukkiness. It takes us to the depths of our personal hell, and holds us prisoner and attempts to annihilate any progress we have made in our recovery. It makes us a captive of our past. How does it do this? It connects with all the other old tapes, and combines to create a rope that pulls you down into the vortex of hate and delusion. It is the core of our dis-ease.

But just saying, "Stop" doesn't take us out of our shame. It just stops us from going deeper into the well. It helps us to know that we are in recovery, and that we have a solution. Our past does not have to have control over our present. Now, we get to inventory our experience, see where it came from, and work on getting back to the surface. It takes time, and effort, but it is possible to change old thinking and reacting to shame when it comes up.

As we inventory, it is important to remember that blame has no place here; but assigning responsibility does. What's the difference, you might ask. Blame keeps us stuck in the past and continues the pain and no progress is made. But, assigning responsibility is necessary for change to take place. "Name it, claim it, and dump it" is one of the tools to assist me in removing the intensity from the event. I get to put a name to what is going on, assign it to the appropriate person/place/thing, and then I get to let it go. Sounds easy, huh? NO!!! It takes time and lots of effort on my part to get to the other side. But, believe me when I tell you, the results have been beyond anything I could have ever imagined. I am no longer pulled miles below the surface and hate myself just because I heard something or saw something that triggered the old shame. Hell of a deal, I tell ya! LOL!

So, rather than just wait for shame to find you, how about an exercise that can help you process them in advance. This doesn't mean you won't have more come up, but you can always write more. We always will have more to overcome. I don't think we ever "arrive", but the journey sure is great!

So, try this 4 column inventory. The first column is where you list the old tape or old idea that brings up shame. In column 2, think about when you first heard or felt this? Who said it? Whose voice do you hear when you hear it today? Remember, it isn't about blame. We are just inventorying the idea. Column 3 represents what does it mean to you? What did it mean originally when you experienced it, and what does it mean now? And the final column is when you get to change the shame; to take away the power it holds over you. This is where you can use positive affirmations to alter the tape, and create a new and positive reality. It takes time, but eventually you will be able to do all of these steps very quickly in your head and process through in just a matter of seconds or minutes what you have held onto for decades….possibly your whole life. It takes practice. And lots of work. But, change is not only possible, but an active part of recovery.

What "shoulds or "shouldn'ts do you hear? I will share a couple of my old ideas, and how the process can work. Of course, how you do this is up to you. I think it is important to work with someone else that is aware of what you are doing, so that they can give you objective feedback. But, whatever works for you. It is your recovery.

Should /Shouldn't	Whose voice?	Meaning?	How to Change
1. I should have more to show for my life than I do.	Society; my mom;	I am a mature woman, and don't have children, don't have tons of money in the bank,	All my needs are met today.

		don't have many of the trappings society says I "should" have in order to be viewed as successful.	
2. I shouldn't feel this way.	My family of origin, society	My feelings are wrong; I should be able to stuff them or just ignore them; they are wrong or bad or not popular	I am ok, just the way I am.

Chapter 9

Positively Amazing

"I am not a has-been. I am a will be." - *Lauren Bacall*

Is it possible to change our reactions to events that seem to attack us daily? Is it possible to get rid of all those old tapes and old messages that keep us from living fully? If so, how do we do that?

First, we need to determine where we need to focus our energy. Where are we lacking our intention? When do we find ourselves feeling horrible when someone says something (whether in person, on tv, or in print), and we feel angry, hurt, resentful, or just tune out? Or end up eating a quart of pecan praline ice cream or going for the third run of the day? Or a billion other ways we stuff our feelings and act as if everything is ok? If I don't look at it, it will go away, right???? NO!

Everyone has their own personal buttons that get pushed. They are instilled deep within us. They might be about finances, relationships, self-image, self-esteem, codependency, or a myriad of other "opportunities" that are just waiting to be engaged.

So, how do we reprogram our buttons? First, we have to learn what they are; then, look for ways to change the energy that comes from them.

What are the messages I say to myself? Do I hear myself say, "You are so stupid? You can't do anything right. Why don't I have (fill in the blank)." Ok, so let's start there.

First: Instead of saying "I am so stupid", say the opposite: "I am intelligent". Basically, list all your old messages, then in the next column just substitute the opposite. Remember, what you say becomes your reality, so be sure you make your new message as positive as is possible for you to make it.

Old message	New message
"I am stupid"	"I am intelligent"
"I can't do anything right"	"I am a capable person"
" I need someone to take care of me"	"I am whole and complete within myself"

These are known as positive affirmations; we are affirming what we want to bring into our lives. It is the re-wiring needed for recovery, to take hold and make the changes we want in our lives. Without the new messages, we just keep being the same person we always were, and will always feel less than, and never reach our potential.

When you create your own affirmations, be sure to keep the words positive: don't use "not", "never", etc. You want to attract the positive energy and not encourage any negativity. An example of this shift from negative to positive: "I am not going to be codependent" would be, "I have healthy boundaries and respect others' boundaries as well".

Here is a list of some other positive affirmations that I have used in the past (and many I still use today!):

- ✓ All my needs are met today.
- ✓ I am whole and complete within myself.
- ✓ I am perfect in all my imperfections.
- ✓ Everything is ok, even though it doesn't feel that way.
- ✓ I am a strong and capable woman in recovery.
- ✓ I am worthy.
- ✓ I am intelligent.

- ✓ I am a good friend.
- ✓ I choose to be in recovery.
- ✓ I am loved.
- ✓ I am a leader.
- ✓ I am capable.

Now, what areas do you need to work on? What will your affirmations be?

Chapter 10

Sanity Savors

"Once you replace negative thoughts with positive ones, you'll start having positive results." - *Willie Nelson*

Well, if you are like me, there are days when everything feels like too much; when there isn't enough coffee in the world to get me through the day. There are times when I find myself taking everything personally and feeling like the world is out to get me. On days like that it is important that I focus on something other than my brain. A friend of mine tells me all the time, "Our brains are for entertainment purposes only." That is so true! So, in order to change our thinking, we need to find something else to focus on; whether it is a thought, phrase, poem, paragraph from your favorite recovery book, or whatever. In early sobriety, I made a book of my favorite passages and poems and kept it beside my phone at my desk at work. Whenever I would get overwhelmed, or had a minute to spare, I would look through the book and feel less anxious and be able to return to what I was doing. I had poetry, prose, recovery slogans, quotes, and even candy wrappers. Back in the '80's there was a candy that had positive sayings inside the wrappers, and each one was a really feel-good quote.

So, I encourage you to create your own Sanity Saver book and keep it near you at work, at home, or wherever. These days, you can just keep it on your phone! We didn't even have cell phones when I got sober! LOL!

Here are some of my favorite sayings, poems, and quotes. I will put many more in the Appendix at the back of the book. I hope you find some that will help you as much as they help me!

"A program is a series of small behaviors that, if repeated consistently will result in new options for a new way of life." – Earnie Larsen

"If you're going through hell, keep going." - Winston Churchill

"It does not matter how slowly you go as long as you do not stop." – Confucius

"What you live with you learn, what you learn you practice, what you practice you become, what you become has consequences." - Earnie Larsen

Dreams *(Langston Hughes - 1902-1967)*

Hold fast to dreams
For if dreams die
Life is a broken-winged bird
That cannot fly.

Hold fast to dreams
For when dreams go
Life is a barren field
Frozen with snow.

I'm Nobody! Who are you? *(Emily Dickinson - 1830-1886)*

I'm nobody! Who are you?
Are you nobody too?
Then there's a pair of us! – don't tell!
They'd banish us, you know!

How dreary to be somebody!
How public, like a frog
To tell your name the livelong day
To an admiring Bog!

Here is my list of my Top 25 favorite slogans:

- ❖ It came to pass, not to stay

- ❖ Grow or Go!

- ❖ Trust the process.

- ❖ What other people think of me is none of my business.

To Thine Own Self Be True

❖ There are two kinds of business: my business and none of my business.

❖ My lack of understanding is my understanding. ~ JoAnn R.

❖ It's a feelings disease therefore it has to be a feelings recovery.

❖ *Pain is inevitable but suffering is optional.

❖ If you have one foot in today and the other foot in tomorrow, you are shitting all over today.

❖ Time Takes Time.

❖ Recovery is a journey, not a destination.

❖ We are as sick as our secrets.

❖ Progress not perfection.

❖ FEAR: False Evidence (or Expectations) Appearing Real.

❖ FEAR: Fuck Everything And Run.

❖ FEAR: Face Everything and Recover.

❖ HALT: Don't get too Hungry, Angry, Lonely or Tired.

❖ If you always do what you've always done, you will always get what you always got.

❖ Focus on the problem and the problem increases; focus on the solution and the solution increases.

❖ RULE 62: don't take yourself so dam seriously.

❖ Pain is the touchstone of growth.

❖ Even if you get the monkey off your back, the circus is still in town.

❖ Not my circus; not my monkeys.

❖ Why doesn't matter; instead, where do we go from here.

❖ If nothing changes nothing changes.

When I say I like the quote, "Pain is inevitable but suffering is optional", I mean that I know that in the course of our life, "stuff" happens that is very painful. It might be trauma from past hurts you experienced or whatever physical, mental, spiritual, or other pain is in your life currently. This is not to be negated at all. But, I think that even the most painful experience has lessons to teach us; and we don't have to hang on to the pains and keep them close to our souls, so they become our identity and never process through the trauma. There are definitely things that produce suffering in our life; but we learn to identify that whatever the situation is that is causing us to suffer, we are NOT our suffering, we are more than that; it isn't our identity, or the main focus of our life.

Chapter 11

Goal setting for Dummies

"By failing to prepare, you are preparing to fail." - *Benjamin Franklin*

First of all, let me say that there are no dummies here! If you are willing to do the work to be different, you are very smart; so smart, in fact, that we will even explain how to be smart in terms of how to set our goals.

Let's be SMART about learning to set goals. Yep. Another acronym. I know you probably hate them, but they are easy to remember, and that is what is important.

When we are taking a journey, how do we get from point A to point B? First we have to know where we want to go, and then we have to figure out how we want to get there. Let's say we want to go to California. Where in California? Once we figure where, let's see how we want to get there. List our options: car, train, plane, bus, RV, hitchhike, motorcycle, bicycle, walk, run, dog sled, and any others we can think of, no matter how crazy or silly. Then, cross off the list those that are not interesting to you, or are unsafe. Also, is there a certain time/day you want to be there? How much money do you have for the trip? This also helps you to look at how you are going to get there. Then, once you get there, where are you going to stay? And how long will you stay? Again, look at finances. What are you going to do while you are there? More money issues to look at in order to work. I know, it can be overwhelming, but that is why it is important to look at every facet and make the best goals to help you be successful.

Now, I know planning a trip may sound corny, but you can bring the same tools into your recovery goals. How do you get to a year of sobriety? Stay sober 24 hours a day for 365 days. How do you become an old-timer? Don't drink and don't die. Well, that sounds silly, I know, and there is SO much more to recovery than just not drinking, but it is an essential start. If alcohol isn't your thing, then just substitute whatever word or phrase fits your situation: codependency; food addiction; gambling; drug addiction; family dysfunction issues; rage addiction; sex addiction; love addiction; depression or other mental health issues; etc.

If you want to change your outcome, you have to change your behaviors. And, anything you change, you have to replace with something else. We aren't Swiss cheese: we can't walk around with gaping holes all through us. So, we work a little at a time, making progress as we go.

SMART:

S = Specific
M = Measurable
A = Achievable or Attainable
R = Realistic
T = Time-based

Specific: You have to identify exactly what you want to work on. There is no room for being vague or covert.

Measurable: How long do you want to work on this? 5 minutes a day for one year, or what???

Achievable or Attainable: Can you achieve or attain your goal in the time you have allowed yourself?

Realistic: Can you really do this? Is it possible?

Time-based: How much time are you willing to allot to this goal?

For example, instead of having "to move to Colorado" as a goal, it's more powerful to use the SMART goal "To have completed my move to Salida, Colorado by May 31, 2022. But, of course, this will only be achieved if a lot of preparation has been completed beforehand!

It is a good idea to put pen to paper (or fingers to keyboard!) to help you with this. Keeping things in your head only leads to anxiety, and we have enough of that already. So, put just jot down a word or two that sums up your goal. Here's an example: Lose weight. Now, that is a worthy goal, but let's explore that further. How much weight? In how much time? When to start? What are your boundaries within this weight loss: no sugar, no fried foods, working out daily for how many minutes, or how many days a week? All of these are important to acknowledge and help you plan out your success. No, know that every plan needs room for change, because, as we all know, life is all about change. So be prepared to adjust as necessary; don't feel you have to adhere perfectly to the plan. We have to learn to be gentle with ourselves as well. Being a strict disciplinarian and harsh critic all wrapped up in one can just be another way to repeat family or societal values that are not conducive to our recovery. Learning balance is one of the huge tools to learn and apply in our journey. But remember, balance isn't all one side or the other. Think of a teeter-totter; you have to go up to come down. And our journeys are like that, too. We don't stay still in one place. We are always moving and changing, so don't get all hung up that you have to be in the same spot with everything. We will change. And, we will be SMART about it!

Chapter 12

Visualize your Reality

"I am not afraid... I was born to do this." Joan of Arc

Create your own path

By placing yourself in your own journey, you get to choose what you want the outcome to be, what you want your day-to-day reality to be. You are the orchestrator of your own destiny. As long as you focus on positives, you get more positive in your life. We attract what we expend....when we focus on the positive, the positive increases; when we focus on the negative, the negative increases; like attracts like. This is known as the law of attraction.

"The law of attraction states that 'like attracts like.'" This means that people with a low frequency – people who are insecure and self-abandoning – attract each other, while people with a high frequency – people who love and value themselves – also attract each other." [v]

Another definition:

"In the New Thought philosophy, the Law of Attraction is the belief that positive or negative thoughts bring positive or negative experiences into a person's life. The belief is based on the ideas that people and their thoughts are made from "pure energy", and that a process of like energy attracting like energy exists through which a person can improve their health, wealth, and personal relationships." [vi]

What do we want for ourselves? If I want to be different, I have to do different things. Remember, one of the definitions of insanity is: "doing the same thing, expecting different results". So, if I want to thrive, I need to stop just getting by. I need to challenge myself, find new interests; maybe even just do ONE THING differently today than I did yesterday. Changing a behavior isn't going to happen overnight, or even in a short time. It takes consistent effort to make a change. And, we have to have a vision of what we want. This has always been hard for me. I want things to be different, but I lack the discipline to make it happen. Then, it becomes a self-fulfilling prophecy of old tapes. And, it supports my poor self-esteem.

So, how do you find a new vision? There are many ways, and you may find ones that work better for you. Here are three options that work for me.

Make a list of what you want in your life. Don't focus on material possessions, but what you want in your life; what you want from your life. Examples might be: happiness, comfort, sobriety, serenity, someone that understands you, being comfortable in your own skin, etc. Whatever you need in order to feel free from the past, your disease, your addiction or whatever is holding you hostage. It may be that you don't want to hate yourself anymore. Or, it might be that you are not willing any longer to resort to negativity as the first line of defense. Write the first things that come to mind. Then, take the list and see what it will take to make them come true. It is always a good idea to ask people you trust to help you answer that part. Don't limit yourself. Think outside the box!

Another tool to use is to make a mission statement for myself. What is my mission in life? What do I want my life to reflect? Personally, I believe my job is to be of service to others. This has really come with some horrible baggage. I thought this meant I had to do FOR others. It is actually the exact opposite. It is respecting their boundaries and sharing *with* them. Helping as I can, but not doing for them the things they can do for themselves. I will never forget when I visited my mom when she was so sick with cancer. She was lying in bed, and I started fluffing her pillows to make her comfortable. She stopped me and said she was already comfortable, and maybe I needed to go find something else to do! I realized that I was the one uncomfortable, not her. I was trying to fix me by fixing her, and that was never my place. I learned so many things from her sickness and death. I miss her, but I would never wish her to still be here in the pain she was experiencing.

And the last instrument to try would be a "vision board". There are tons of ways to do this, but the way that I like is to get a stack of magazines, a piece of poster board, a glue stick, scissors, and sit down on your bed or the kitchen table (or wherever you are most comfortable) and start looking through magazines. Find words, pictures, quotes, cartoons, anything that catches your eye. Look for things that you want in your life, or that you want your life to represent. What are things you like or are interested in doing?

Don't worry about how everything is going to fit together, just cut them out and put in a pile. (Oh, and from experience....you might want to look at the back of the page before you cut to see if there is something you might want even more!) Once you have all the items cut out, get your poster board. Just start putting them on the board. Don't glue them down yet! Arrange, rearrange, shift, tilt, change until you like where they are; then glue! You can even decorate with glitter or stickers or anything you want! It is YOUR vision board. There is no wrong or right way to do it! Just like there is no wrong or right way to be in recovery. The journey is all yours. And no one can take it away from you. That is one thing that makes it so wonderful and amazing.

Whatever, and however you find your vision, just know that it is yours and yours alone. You don't have to define it for anyone else, or even share it with anyone else if you don't want to. And if you do decide to share it, they may not be able to understand it; not because they don't want to, but because they haven't walked your path. Remember, we each come to recovery with our own experiences; and even though there may be many things in common, there is also much that is uniquely ours.

Recovery is about learning to be centered in self, rather than self-centered. We go from, "This is all about ME ME ME!" to "This is MINE: I take ownership of my part in my life." This used to really confuse me when I was early in my journey. I kept hearing, "It's a selfish program", and I thought that was a bad thing. I was always told that being selfish was the opposite of what we were "supposed" to be; that sharing was what was important, and being selfish made you a bad kid. But, that isn't what is meant at all by that phrase. Instead, it just means I am looking at me, and I take responsibility for myself, my actions, reactions, and the consequences of my behaviors. I don't blame anyone or anything for what has happened in the past, nor give away my power of choices for the future. As Doris used to tell me all the time, "if anything were different, everything would be different; one less drink, one more drink, and I wouldn't be here." I know this to be a truth for me. Life happens. It isn't all pretty and happy. There is pain. This is true even after we get into recovery. We just learn how to grow through it, instead of letting it determine how and who we are. We aren't immune to life; that is what we did before recovery. Today, I get to feel it all, even though sometimes it sucks.

Chapter 13

Creativity – find a way to say it

I tell you, we are here on Earth to fart around, and don't let anybody tell you different. ~ Kurt Vonnegut

One of the many important lessons I have learned, is that there is more to living than just going to work, coming home, fixing dinner, going to a meeting, watching TV and then going to bed. Then, get up the next day and do the same thing over and over and over again. This leads to boredom and anxiety, and keeps us stuck in our dis-ease. There has to be a part of our existence where we actually use a part of our brain that taps into our soul. It may be music or art or photography or any number of things. If you are unsure what your creative talent is, try several! See what interests you. Try something new. One thing to remember is to be good to yourself. If you try something you have never done before, you probably are not going to be an expert or a professional initially. Give yourself a chance to get comfortable with this new opportunity; know that it is likely that you might have some difficulty initially, but as the old saying goes, "repetition strengthen and confirms". To me this means try and try again. The more I practice, the better I will get. I never will be perfect, so I avoid the adage, "practice makes perfect". That doesn't work for me. It seems to set me up to fail, so I avoid it. But I know I must repeat things in order to learn them.

One of the ways to find out what you like is look around you and see who you enjoy. Is it an artist, musician, sports personality, writer, comedian, actor/actress, or who? What are some of your interests? I personally love music. I come from a long line of music lovers. According to my grandma, one of our ancestors was a minstrel man who went from town to town via covered wagon. It kind of reminds me of the character from the Wizard of Oz. And he did live in Kansas. Hmmm. Just kidding. No relation I am sure!

So, how do I find out what I might want to try? First, write a list of things you like. Break them down into categories, such as:

Sports
Art/Crafts
Writing
Outdoors/Gardening
Music
Theater/Movies
Collecting
Photography
Sewing/Quilting/Crotchet/Knitting
Animals
Computers
Science

Education/Learning
Volunteering
(And many other topics – See Appendix #4 for more suggestions.)

Then check whether the activity is one you would observe or participate in. After that, see what it will take to learn how to do the action. YouTube is a great way to learn all kinds of things; practically anything on earth! And a lot of things you never even knew existed!

Next, divide your list into long term and short term goals. You may want to try something that doesn't take long to learn initially, so that you will have a faster sense of accomplishment, but that is up to you. Just the process of doing something is what is important here. Learning allows your brain to stay alert and make positive changes in other areas of your recovery. Also, when you are being creative and learning something new, it keeps you occupied on a solution, instead of the problem that is often first and foremost in our head.

Take your time and learn something new. Or re-learn something you haven't done in a long time. Often in our disease, whether it is co-dependency, addiction or whatever is standing in our way from being the best we can be, we stop taking care of ourselves. Find a hobby, a new interest, anything that helps you use your brain. And don't feel like you have to be perfect or do it perfectly, especially the first time. It takes time to learn something new. And, sometimes it gets messy. So be nice to yourself; and treat yourself as you would treat a friend you care about. Because you are that friend!

CODA

In musical terminology a coda is the section at the end of a composition that sums up the piece and helps to bring everything together for closure. And, since I did major in music in college, I thought this might be an appropriate term to call my "final thoughts" summary.

I want to remind the reader that this book is based on my experience, strength, and hope from over 37 years of recovery. I don't profess to say that everything works the same way for everybody, or in the same time frame. It takes consistent effort and practice of the tools discussed to make lasting changes; however, I do believe you will find that progress will be made early on. Just keep working; and using the tools will become second nature to you. Remember, time takes time.

Getting comfortable with the inventory process will make all the difference in your recovery. By learning how to listen to your inner voice and work through the old tapes and messages, you will find you have created a firm foundation for your life; and, therefore, you will be less likely to return to old, self-defeating behaviors.

Understanding your own feelings dictionary will empower you to become an emotionally stronger person. No longer will you feel lost and confused, just because you don't know what you are feeling. You will be able to stand tall and strong against the powerful winds that life sends your way.

I know one of the most powerful tools I have ever learned is to treat myself like I would treat my best friend. This includes, but is not limited to the following: how I talk to myself determines how I feel about myself; when to surrender, and when to stand up for myself; the importance of accepting where I am, and learning how to utilize mindfulness techniques when I get overwhelmed, anxious, or just out of sorts; knowing that my feelings are not facts, and I don't have to act on every thought. These, and so many more tools are how I choose to make the most of, because I want to be the best I possibly can be...today, and every day.

And, that is my hope for you as well. Just don't give up; no matter what!

Appendices:

1. Weapons of our Disease and

   Tools of our Recovery

2. Slogans and Acronyms

3. Quotes

4. Activities and Interests List

5. References/Footnotes

Appendix 1:

Weapons of our Disease:	Tools of our Recovery:
Shame	Willingness
Self-pity	Honesty
Rage	Compassion
Depression	Self-love
Lies/Self-deceit	Positive Affirmations
Arrogance/Ego	&Self Talk/Sanity
Co-dependency	Savers
False Pride	Trust in the process,
Distrust	trust of others
Fear	Sharing
Internalized Self-phobia	Open-mindedness
Justification	Courage
Rationalization	Determination
Intellectualization	Inventory
Procrastination	Risk
	Healthy Boundaries
	Acceptance
	Introspection

On the Beam	Off the Beam	12 Principles
Faith	Fear	Honesty
Hope	Worry	Hope
Charity	Anger	Faith
Aspiration	Jealousy	Courage
Patience	Criticism	Integrity
Sympathy	Vanity	Willingness
Non-Interference	Hatred	Humility
Kindness	Envy	Brotherly Love
Courage	Hypocrisy	Discipline
Forgiveness	Prejudice	Continuity of Effort
Duty	Selfishness	Awareness
Love	Greed	Service

There are many more tools, and you will add to your own list as you continue your path in recovery.

Appendix 2:

SLOGANS AND ACRONYMS

Here is a short alphabetical list of slogans heard around the rooms. Enjoy!

- A journey of a thousand miles begins with the first step.

- This is a simple program for complicated people.

- We have to act our way into right thinking, rather than think our way into right action.

- Alcoholism is an equal opportunity destroyer.

- Bring the body and the mind will follow.

- Burdens are lighter when they are shared.

- Denial is not a river in Egypt, but you can drown in it.

- Don't compare – Identify

- Faith without works is dead.

- Fear is the darkroom where negatives are developed.

- This is a formula for failure: try to please everyone.

- Guilt is the gift that keeps on giving.

- I don't drink....NO MATTER WHAT

- If it's mentionable, it's manageable.

- If you want what we have and you're willing to go to any lengths to get it

- Insanity is defined as doing the same thing over and over again expecting different results.

- It is not the experience of today that drives people mad, it is remorse of yesterday and the dread of tomorrow.

- Minds are like parachutes----they won't work unless they're open.

- More will be revealed

- Move a muscle, change a thought.

- One drink is too many and thousand not enough.

- Pain is the touchstone of growth.

- Pain shared is pain lessened

- People who are wrapped up in themselves make a very small package indeed...

- Progress not perfection.

- Recovery is a process.

- Repetition strengthens and confirms and faith comes naturally.

- Restraint of pen and tongue (and fingers on keyboard!).

- Serenity is not freedom from the storm but peace amid the storm.

- Shut the fuck up (Short version of the Serenity Prayer). Helen D.

- Sick and tired of being sick and tired.

- Slogans are wisdom written in shorthand.

- Take what you want and leave the rest.

- The road to resentment is paved with expectation.

- There are two days in every week which we have no control over----yesterday and tomorrow.

- There is no chemical solution to a spiritual problem.

- There's a difference between being lonely and being alone.

- To keep it, you have to give it away.

- We teach people how to treat us.

- We're all here because we're not all there.

- When all else fails, work with another.

- When in doubt DON'T.

- Wherever you go, there you are.

- You are not required to like it; you're only required to DO it.

- You can't pour from an empty cup.

- You may not be thinking about the drink, but the drink is always thinking of you.

Acronyms:

CANT: Convenient Answer Not True

FEAR: False Evidence (or Expectations) Appearing Real.

FEAR: Face Everything And Recover

FEAR: Fuck Everything And Run.

FEAR: Frustration, Ego, Anxiety, Resentment.

FINE: Full of Fear, Into Self, Negative and Egotistical

FINE: Fucked up, Insecure, Negative and Emotional

FOMON: Fear of Missing Out

HALT: Don't get too Hungry, Angry, Lonely or Tired.

HOPE: Happy Our Program Exists

KISS: Keep It Short and Simple

Appendix 3:

QUOTES:

Here are some of my favorite quotes. They help me stay in a positive place, and sometimes challenge me to be a better person.

My mission in life is not merely to survive, but to thrive; and to do so with some passion, some compassion, some humor, and some style. - Maya Angelou

If you're going through hell, keep going. -Winston Churchill

Only I can change my life. No one can do it for me. - Carol Burnett

With the new day comes new strength and new thoughts. -Eleanor Roosevelt

It always seems impossible until it's done. - Nelson Mandela

I am not a has-been. I am a will be. -Lauren Bacall

It does not matter how slowly you go as long as you do not stop. Confucius

Do the difficult things while they are easy and do the great things while they are small. A journey of a thousand miles must begin with a single step. - Lao Tzu

Do not wait; the time will never be 'just right.' Start where you stand, and work with whatever tools you may have at your command, and better tools will be found as you go along. - George Herbert

There's only one rule you need to remember: laugh at everything and forget everybody else! It sound egotistical, but it's actually the only cure for those suffering from self-pity. - Anne Frank

I am only one, but still I am one. I cannot do everything, but still I can do something; and because I cannot do everything I will not refuse to do the something that I can do, - Helen Keller Always remember you are braver than you believe, stronger than you seem, smarter than you think and twice as beautiful as you've ever imagined. - Dr. Seuss

Don't think, just do. - Horace

We may encounter many defeats but we must not be defeated. - Maya Angelou

Growth itself contains the germ of happiness. - Pearl S. Buck

Some of us think holding on makes us strong; but sometimes it is letting go. - Hermann Hesse

A single twig breaks, but the bundle of twigs is strong. - Tecumseh

That which does not kill us makes us stronger. - Friedrich Nietzsche

Nobody can hurt me without my permission. - Mahatma Gandhi

Suffering isn't ennobling, recovery is. - Christiaan Barnard

Things do not change; we change. - Henry David Thoreau

What lies behind you and what lies in front of you, pales in comparison to what lies inside of you. - Ralph Waldo Emerson

There is a sacredness in tears. They are not the mark of weakness, but of power. They speak more eloquently than ten thousand tongues. They are the messengers of overwhelming grief, of deep contrition, and of unspeakable love. - Washington Irving

Mistakes are part of the dues one pays for a full life. - Sophia Loren

You only live once, but if you do it right, once is enough. – Mae West

Let us so live that when we come to die even the undertaker will be sorry. – Mark Twain

Appendix 4:

ACTIVITIES AND INTERESTS

Here is just a sampling of ideas to help you chose to learn something new or renew an old love. For more ideas, check out Youtube, your local community college, or a Massive Open Online Courses (MOOCs) such as Coursera.org. Also, check your local newspaper for events. You never know what you might find! See if your city has a community maker space, community chorus/band, community art school, or whatever! Don't let your brain limit your choices! Try several! See what makes you feel good!

- ➢ art restoration
- ➢ art: paint (watercolor, acrylic, oil, tole, etc.)
- ➢ cake decorating
- ➢ calligraphy
- ➢ candle making
- ➢ Computer: repair, assemble, write blog, app design, etc.

- ➢ cooking / baking/ chef
- ➢ crocheting, cross stitch, knitting, weaving, embroidery, etc.
- ➢ dancing/choreography
- ➢ decorating; home, clothes, etc.
- ➢ dried flowers crafts
- ➢ flower arranging
- ➢ furniture making /painting /repair
- ➢ gardening: flowers, vegetables, hydroponic, etc.
- ➢ gift basket making
- ➢ home improvement
- ➢ improv comedy, standup comedy
- ➢ jewelry making
- ➢ magic tricks
- ➢ music: play instrument, write songs, etc
- ➢ origami
- ➢ photography
- ➢ pottery
- ➢ rug making

- scrapbooking
- sculpting: clay, sand, etc.
- sewing, quilting, clothes designing, etc.
- singing
- soap making
- sports: watch or play
- teaching
- volunteering
- woodworking
- wreath making
- writing: a poem, prose, song, blog, book, etc.

REFERENCES/FOOTNOTES

i. https://www.dictionary.com/browse/defect

ii. https://www.dictionary.com/browse/character

iii. https://www.dictionary.com/browse/boundary

iv. https://www.dictionary.com/browse/wall

v. *"Relationships: Why You Attract Who You Attract"* by Margaret Paul, PhD, Contributor, Best-selling author, seminar leader and co-creator of Inner Bonding, Huffington Post, May 15, 2012 https://www.huffpost.com/entry/relationship-advice_b_1516235#:~:text=The%20law%20of%20attraction%20states,%2D%2D%20also%20attract%20each%20other)

vi. https://en.wikipedia.org/wiki/Law_of_attraction_(New_Thought)

ABOUT THE AUTHOR

Sandy Jolley lives just outside of Winston Salem, NC. She lives with her partner and best friend, Ben Branch surrounded by trees and nature. She has been sober since August 4, 1984. She loves cooking, music, photography, nature, and watching movies.

Made in the USA
Columbia, SC
29 December 2021